TOM COCKLE

WAR
PHOTOGRAPHER

peko
PUBLISHING

INTRODUCTION

© PeKo Publishing Kft.

Published by
PeKo Publishing Kft.
8360 Keszthely, Bessenyei György utca 37., Hungary
Email: info@pekobooks.com
www.pekobooks.com

Responsible publisher
Péter Kocsis

Author
Tom Cockle

Printed in Hungary

Photos
Péter Kocsis

First published
2019

ISBN 978-615-5583-19-3

All rights reserved. No parts of this publication may be reproduced, or transmitted in any form or by any means, electronic or mechanical, including photocopying, recording or by any information storage and retrieval system, without permission from the Publisher in writing.

This new photo book series presents you various selections of rare wartime photographs. They will be selected based on numerous subjects. Each volume introduces photographs from battles, operations, vehicles or complete photo albums from soldiers who fought in World War Two.

This book illustrates photos from an unidentified German Sturmartillerist of the Sturmgeschütz-Abteilung 189 from his service in the Reichsarbeitsdienst, to his Sturmartillerie training, combat in Russia and finally to officer school.

All German men aged 18 to 25 were required to serve six months in the Reichsarbeitsdienst (Reich Labor Service, or RAD) before they began their military service. A group of exuberant young men are shown arriving at their destination to begin their service. They have been issued new uniforms and pose for a photo at the gate to the camp where they will spend their next six months. The sign over the gate reads, 'Reichsarbeitsdienstabteilung 1/220' with 'Philipp der Großmütige' below. Born in Marburg in 1504, Philipp was a leading figure of the Protestant Reformation. Our unknown soldier is the tall man with the glasses.

They wore uniforms similar to the German Army but with different insignia. A swastika armband was worn on the left arm with the RAD arm badge, a shovelhead with the group and detachment numbers, sewn above it. Our unknown soldier is wearing a Nazi Party badge on his breast pocket. In the right photo, his comrade is wearing the SA Sports Badge in silver, the Sports Badge in bronze and Hitler Youth pin on his tunic.

The RAD was a paramilitary organization and the men were trained in marching and close order drill. The RAD had a special belt buckle featuring the swastika in the center of an upturned shovelhead inside a wreath of wheat stalks. The cap badge was a shovelhead with a swastika and two wheat stalks arranged in a 'V' below. A system of rank shoulder straps similar to that of the army was also used. The man on the left is wearing the shoulder straps for a RAD-Obertruppführer.

A rare experimental Beobachtungswagen constructed on the chassis of the 0 Serie D 6 Fahrgestell, and a precursor to the Sd.Kfz.253. It is painted in the two-tone dunkelgrau Nr.46 and dunkelbraun Nr.45 paint scheme that was authorized on 7 November 1938. The white wreath emblem encircling a red bombard on the fender indicates it was attached to the Artillerie-Lehr-Regiment at Jüterbog. Our man is shown wearing headphones inside the vehicle in his new German army uniform.

According to K.St.N.445, the Batterietrupp was provided with two Kfz.15 Nachrichtungkraftwagen signaling service cars. These two are Horch 830 B1 medium standard cross-country cars that have been fitted with radio equipment to perform its role. In the background we can see one of the experimental Beobachtungswagen and what looks to be two Mercedes-Benz 170 VK Kfz.2.

Above Left: A studio portrait of our soldier in his new German army uniform. Unusually, it doesn't have the dark blue-green collar that was standard at the time and appears on his uniform in later photos.
Above Middle: Posing for a picture at a viewpoint overlooking a river somewhere in Germany.
Above Right: On sentry duty in his new field grey assault gun uniform most likely at Schweinfurt.

A batterie of six guns is assembled in the parade ground along with its support vehicles on 23 March 1941 in Schweinfurt. According to K.St.N.445 dated 11 November 1939, each Sturmbatterie was authorized six Sturmgeschütz, five le.gep.Beob.Kw. (Sd.Kfz.253) armored observation vehicles, six le.gep.Mun.Tr.Kw. (Sd.Kfz.252) armored ammunition carriers and three m.gep.M.T.W. (Sd.Kfz.251) half-tracks along with several unarmored support vehicles.

A new StuG.III Ausf.B on the parade ground at Schweinfurt. Improvements made over the Ausf.A are the 40cm wide tracks, here without slots for ice sprags called Hammerstollen on the ends, cast drive sprocket, 95mm wide road wheels, relocated front return roller and the addition of an armored cover on the smoke candle discharger on the rear of the engine deck. Note the nonstandard brush guards over the lights and horn.

Two new StuG.III Ausf.B from 3.Battr. StuG.Abt.200 followed by three le.gep.Mun.Tr.Kw. (Sd.Kfz.252) and several trucks roll down a country road near Schweinfurt during training on 29 April 1941. The StuG.III Ausf.B was armed with a 7.5cm KwK L/24 along with two 9mm M.P. for crew protection. The front and rear fenders are outlined in white to improve their visibility at night.

Another StuG.III Ausf.B photographed on 11 May 1941 during training. The repositioned front return roller can be clearly seen. The access hatches in the glacis in front of the driver are in the open position, probably to provide more ventilation for him.

Left: Our unknown soldier dressed in his field grey assault gun uniform including his Stahlhelm and personal P08 Luger pistol.
Above Right: A crewmember stands in front of the headquarters of 3.Battr.Sturm-Gesch.Erz.Abt.200 in Schweinfurt. He is wearing a Hitler Youth Proficiency Award for members 10-14 years old.
Below Middle: Sturmartillerie crews dressed in their field grey assault gun uniforms march across the Rathausplatz in Schweinfurt on 20 April 1941.

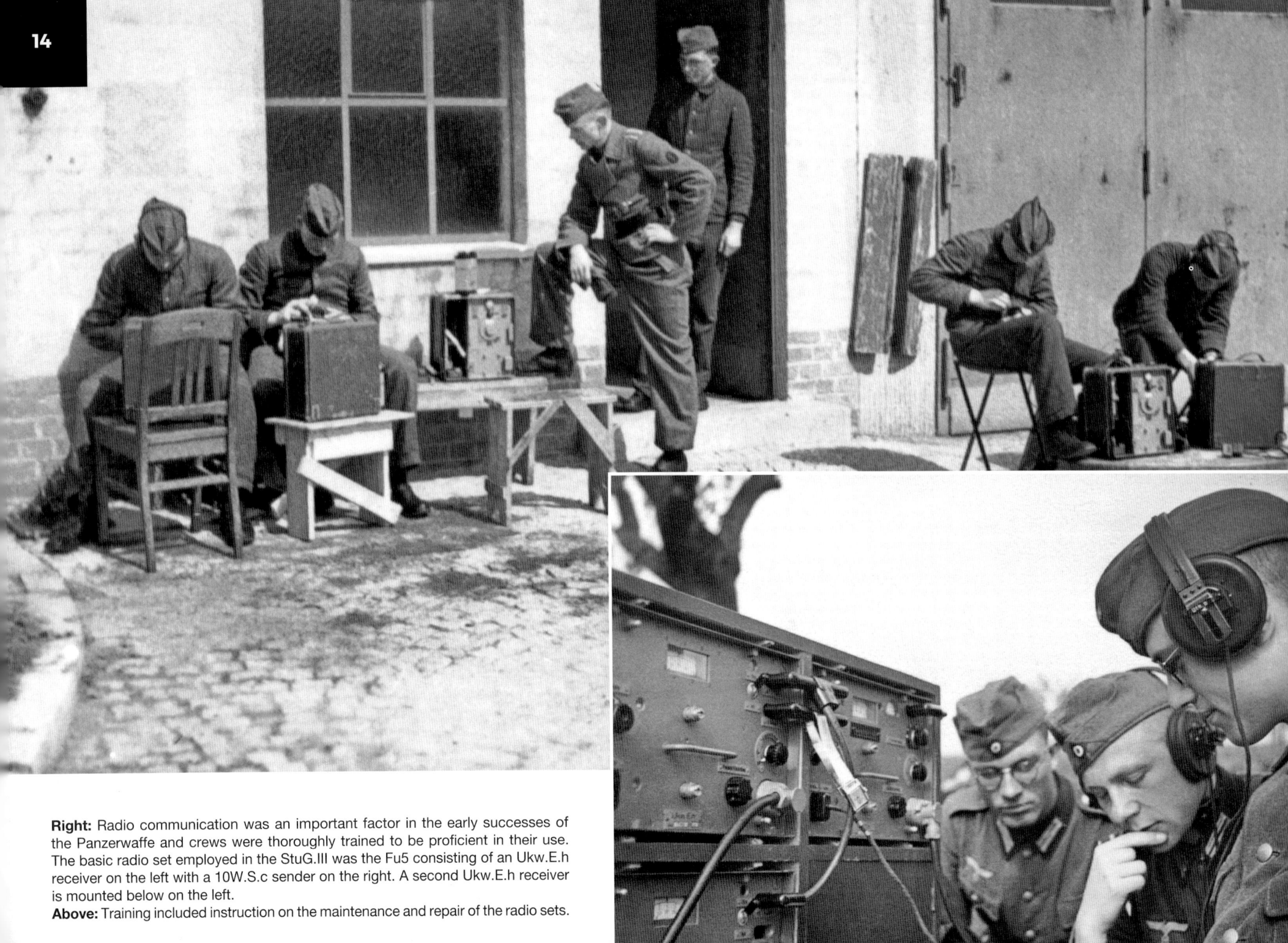

Right: Radio communication was an important factor in the early successes of the Panzerwaffe and crews were thoroughly trained to be proficient in their use. The basic radio set employed in the StuG.III was the Fu5 consisting of an Ukw.E.h receiver on the left with a 10W.S.c sender on the right. A second Ukw.E.h receiver is mounted below on the left.
Above: Training included instruction on the maintenance and repair of the radio sets.

On 9 July 1941, StuG.Abt.189 was formed with three batteries and sent to Russia, reaching the Vitebsk area in August where it was assigned to IX.Armee-Korps. They were issued with new StuG.III Ausf.D, identifiable here by the wooden antenna trough installed on the left side of the engine deck. The guns within each battery were identified with letters, following the practice of the artillery branch. Alkett produced 150 Ausf.D from May to September 1941.

Above: The le.gep.Mun.Tr.Kw. (Sd.Kfz.252) armored ammunition carriers are lined up behind the guns and also have the letter that corresponds to their assigned gun painted on the side. Note the specially made canvas covers over the opening in the roof for the gun sight that are held in place with leather straps inserted through tie downs welded to the roof plate. Also note the different placement of the collar patches on each man's tunic.

Right: Assault guns and transport vehicles travel by rail into Russia in the summer of 1941. The unit emblem, a shield consisting of the image of half a knight on the left side and half an eagle on the right, has been painted on the left fender. At least one reference depicts the left side of the shield in red but it is unknown if the color was the same for each battery.

This StuG.III Ausf.D has attracted a large crowd of onlookers after becoming stuck in a small stream. The unit's vehicles carried a white outline Balkenkreuz painted on both sides and rear. The white circle has a darker color painted inside and likely indicates it is a command vehicle. The top of the Rbl.F.32 gun sight can be seen sticking up from the roof in front of the Scherenfernrohr 14 scissors periscope in the commander's hatch.

The opposite side of the same StuG.III Ausf.D in the previous photo. Some officers have now appeared on the scene as one of the crewmen prepares to attach a tow cable to the front of the immobilized vehicle. Extracting the 20-ton vehicle will not be an easy task.

Above: One of the crewmen prepares a meal over an open brazier behind the same vehicle shown in the previous photos. The white outline Balkenkreuz has been painted on the armored cover on the smoke candle rack and the white circle is repeated on the cover of the crank starter port in the rear plate. In addition to the extra road wheels carried, four lengths of the new 40cm track with the slots in the ends for Hammerstollen are attached to the rear.

Right: A crewman relaxes on an old leather truck seat in front of an elaborate log shelter that features a door probably taken from the same truck. The top has been covered with sod and a Zeltbahn shelter quarter covers what is probably a leaky spot. Some sort of matting on the ground leads up to the doorway.

The crew of gun 'B' have set themselves up next to a farmhouse and constructed a dugout for protection. The man on the left is wearing one-piece coveralls while our man standing in the trench is wearing his regulation field grey assault gun uniform. The Feldwebel and other man sitting on the bench seem to be wearing the drill fatigue uniform that was often dyed reed green and used during the first summer on the Russian Front until proper summer uniforms were available.

This battle damaged StuG.III Ausf.D has been immobilized while crossing a shallow river and is waiting to be pulled out by another vehicle. A white outline Balkenkreuz can be faintly seen on the sloping side plate and a 'C' denoting the gun's position within the battery is painted on the armored pannier protecting the vehicle commander's radio. Logs have been placed on the riverbank in front to help carry the weight of the vehicle over the soft ground.

In this view, the damaged StuG.III Ausf.D has been successfully pulled ashore.

Left: A close-up of a StuG.III Ausf.D showing our man in the loader/radio operator's position wearing the ribbon of the Iron Cross Second Class in his lapel. Unusually, there are no patches sewn on his collar. The gun commander, Oberleutnant Wilhelm von Malachowski, who was also commander of 2./StuG.Abt.189, is on the right.
Above: The vehicle pauses for a rest in a grassy field while some supplies are brought up in a horse drawn cart.
Below: One of the le.gep.Mun.Tr.Kw. (Sd.Kfz.252) armored ammunition carriers is shown here moving through a muddy field. The only marking appears to be the unit emblem painted on the left front plate and an indistinguishable marking on the right. The left side of the shield in the emblem appears to be a light color indicating there might have been different colors for each battery.

A newly white washed StuG.III Ausf.D sits in front of a house during the first winter in Russia. The unit emblem on the left fender has been neatly painted around and it is clear the left side is a dark color. On the right fender, the tactical sign for a self-propelled artillery unit has been left in the original dark grey paint.

In this view of the same vehicle on the previous page, we can see that the winter white wash has been applied to the superstructure and lower hull front, and probably rear, but not on the lower hull sides or running gear, possibly to conserve paint. A larger dark grey Balkenkreuz has been left on the side after the white outline has been painted over. Note the two horns that have been installed on the front fender.

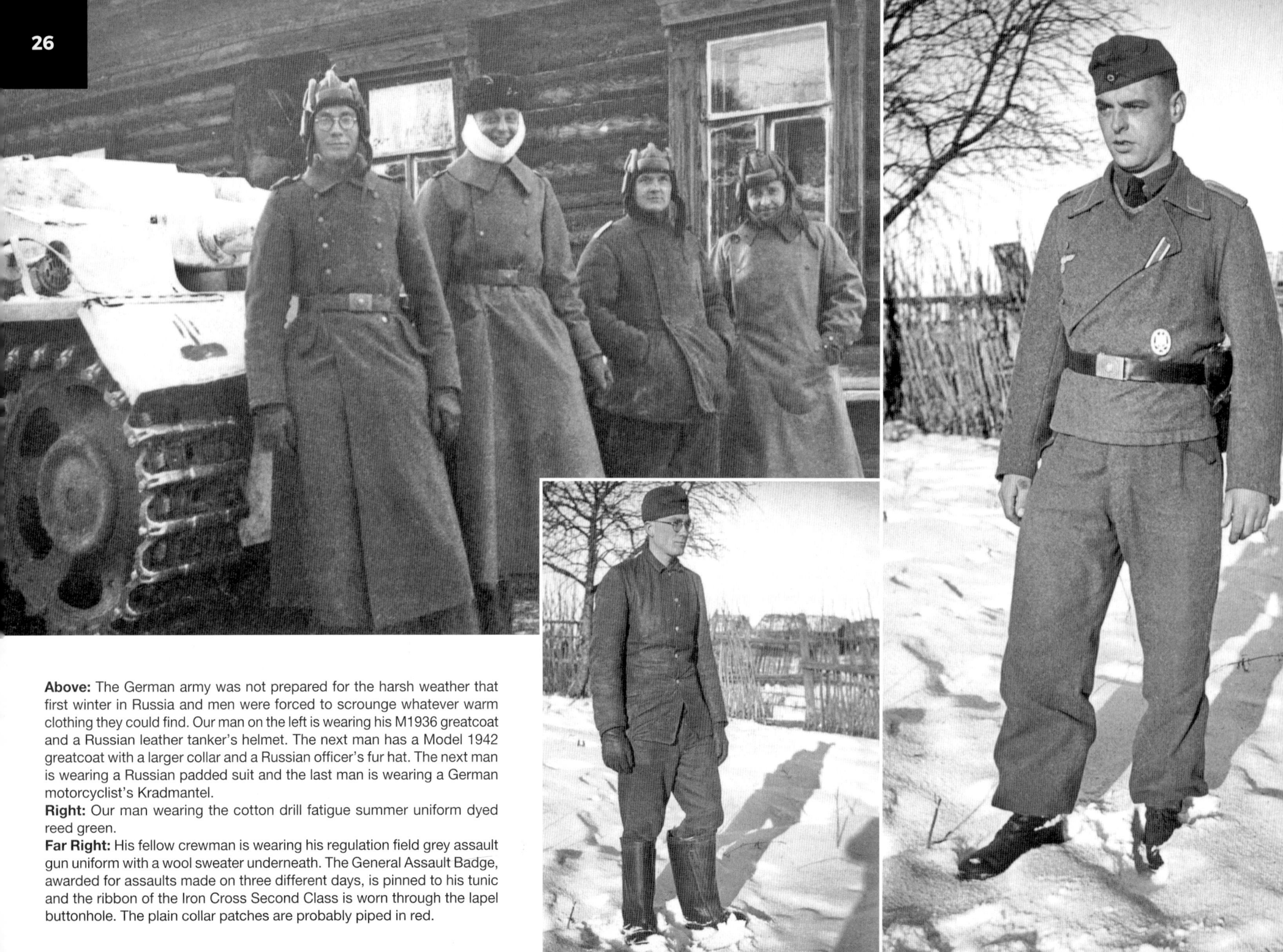

Above: The German army was not prepared for the harsh weather that first winter in Russia and men were forced to scrounge whatever warm clothing they could find. Our man on the left is wearing his M1936 greatcoat and a Russian leather tanker's helmet. The next man has a Model 1942 greatcoat with a larger collar and a Russian officer's fur hat. The next man is wearing a Russian padded suit and the last man is wearing a German motorcyclist's Kradmantel.

Right: Our man wearing the cotton drill fatigue summer uniform dyed reed green.

Far Right: His fellow crewman is wearing his regulation field grey assault gun uniform with a wool sweater underneath. The General Assault Badge, awarded for assaults made on three different days, is pinned to his tunic and the ribbon of the Iron Cross Second Class is worn through the lapel buttonhole. The plain collar patches are probably piped in red.

Above and Below Left: Elaborately prepared graves for Wachtmeister Hans Tabbert and Kanonier Josef Arenz from 2./Sturmgesch.Abt.189. The date of death, 12.11.41, can be faintly made out on the right marker.

Above: For the living, life must carry on. Poorly dressed for the cold weather, our man and his comrades appear to be bringing hot food carried on a Russian horse drawn sleigh.

Left: Two new StuG.III Ausf.E, identifiable by the longer armored radio compartments on each side and smaller hinges for the bow access hatches, stand by while a group of officers confer on the road beside them. Just ahead, an ammunition trailer can be seen, likely towed by a le.gep.Mun.Tr.Kw. (Sd.Kfz.252). Production of the StuG.III Ausf.E commenced in September 1941 with 272 produced until March 1942.
Right: A StuG.III Ausf.D in the same column of vehicles. The crew appears much better dressed for the winter conditions than previously seen. Note the dark circle on the side of the pannier, possibly indicating it is the same vehicle we saw that was stuck in the small stream.
Below Right: The assembled battery has stopped on a road through a Russian town. The last vehicle is still moving so perhaps they have just arrived. As part of the IX.Armee-Korps, 2./StuG.Abt.189 took part in the winter battles around Rzhev in the first months of 1942.

The commander of 2./StuG.Abt.189, Oberleutnant Wilhelm von Malachowski was awarded the Knight's Cross on 9 February 1942 for his actions during the winter battles. He is seen here with 'der Spiess', (regimental Sargent-Major) as indicated by the double row of braid on his sleeves and holding the rank of Hauptfeldwebel or Hauptwachmeister. He also has a double braid bar on his shoulder straps indicating he is an Offizier Anwärter, or officer aspirant. A StuG.III Ausf.E is on the right.

Above: Oberleutnant von Malachowski standing in front of another headquarters building with the battery emblem hanging on the wall beside him. Besides his Knight's Cross at his neck, he also wears the ribbon of the Iron Cross Second Class in his lapel, the Iron Cross First Class, the General Assault Badge and the Wound Badge in silver for three or four wounds.
Right: The emblem of Stu.Gesch.Abt.189 neatly painted on wood with a half-round border of birch logs.

Left: A view of the battery headquarters with von Malachowski's StuG.III Ausf.E parked in front, although at a later date as the tow cable is now hanging on an 'S' hook from the spare tracks stowed on the back of the engine deck. Warmer weather has come and the leaves are starting to appear on the trees.

Above: Two Unteroffizier relax and enjoy a cigarette and some conversation. Both are wearing the field grey assault gun uniform with skull insignia on their collar patches and Iron Cross Second Class ribbons in their lapels. They also have a double braid bar on their shoulder straps indicating both are Offizier Anwärter. The man on the right also has the General Assault Badge pinned to his tunic.

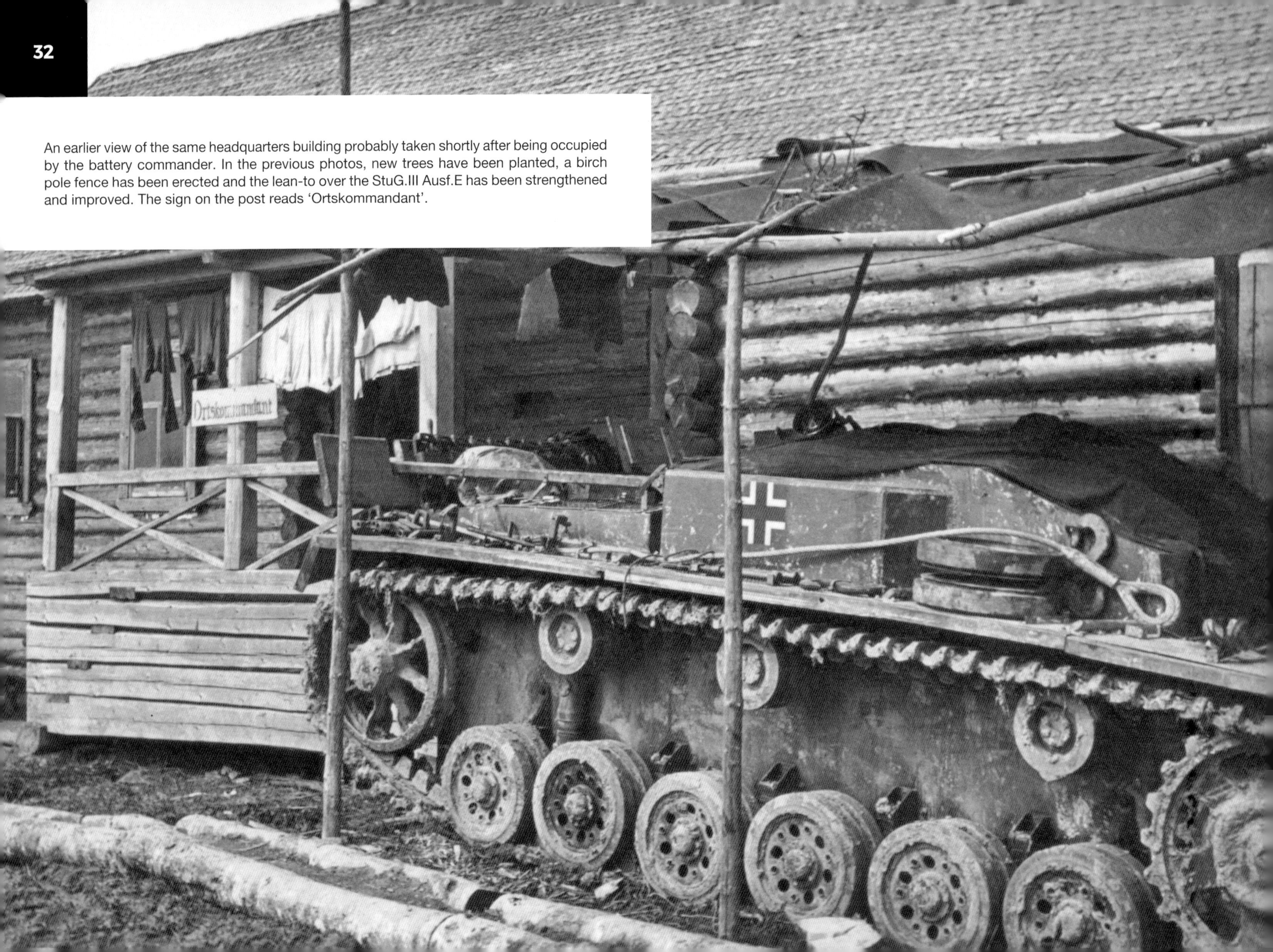

An earlier view of the same headquarters building probably taken shortly after being occupied by the battery commander. In the previous photos, new trees have been planted, a birch pole fence has been erected and the lean-to over the StuG.III Ausf.E has been strengthened and improved. The sign on the post reads 'Ortskommandant'.

Now that warmer weather has arrived, the crews get to work covering the winter white wash camouflage paint with a new coat of dark grey laboriously applied with a brush. This is the command StuG.III Ausf.D that was previously seen bogged down in a stream.

Our man continues with the new paint on the front of the StuG.III Ausf.D. The large hatch hinges were replaced with smaller internal hinges with the introduction of the StuG.III Ausf.E.

Two photos of a crew relaxing during a break in the fighting. In the left photo, the man on the left is wearing the General Assault Badge and the wound Badge in black for one or two wounds, The Leutnant has the General Assault badge just visible behind his left cuff as does the man on the right. All are wearing the ribbon of the Iron Cross Second Class in their lapel. In the background is a French built Renault AHR 5-t truck.

A hot meal is about to be served from a Gulaschkanone, or mobile field kitchen, invented in Germany in 1892. It received its unlikely name due to its resemblance to an artillery piece when the chimney was removed and stowed for transport.

Left: A StuG.III Ausf.E parked next to a log barn. A bunch of small poles have been leaned up against it to help disguise the shape from Russian aircraft flying over. The Feldwebel sitting on the gun, probably the gun commander, is wearing the ribbon of the Iron Cross Second Class in his lapel. Note the spare road wheel stowed on the side of the superstructure, the spare track bar on the front and the lucky horseshoe attached to the headlight cover.
Above: A group of the men have gathered around a table to relax and enjoy some music accompanied by an accordion. Whenever the troops were stationed in the rear for any period of time, they worked to better their living conditions by building tables, chairs and benches with materials at hand like the birch logs seen here.

This is the same StuG.III Ausf.E seen in the previous photo. The added spare track bar can be more clearly seen here and the crewmen have also added extra spare tracks on top of the driver's position, over the gun and probably on the right side as well. Note the added electric horn on the right fender. The gun in the background has been similarly equipped.

The battery headquarters StuG.III Ausf.D is having some maintenance on its final drives, which has required removal of the drive sprocket and idler. The command pennant slipped over the top of the antenna should be artillery red with a black cross. Again, branches and a tarp have been used in an attempt to conceal the vehicle's shape from the air. Maintenance in the field was a difficult task that needed to be performed in all types of weather.

Right: A le.gep.Mun.Tr.Kw. (Sd.Kfz.252) armored ammunition carrier appears to be assisting two Opel Blitz S-type 3-t trucks across a muddy field. This would have severely taxed the power train for the vehicle as it was originally designed with a towing capacity of 1-t.
Above: The driver smiles for the camera after stopping. Markings include the white outline Balkenkreuz and the letter 'C' indicating the gun to which it was attached in the battery. An illegible series of letters or numbers can be seen below. A turn signal was originally attached to the angle frame fixed to the side.

Two of the battery's le.gep.Mun.Tr.Kw. (Sd.Kfz.252) armored ammunition carriers have stopped in an open field during their advance. An Sd.Ah.32 ammunition trailer can be seen in the background between them. Both vehicles and the trailer have the unit shield emblem painted on the rear and the right vehicle has an 'A' painted in white in front of the white outline Balkenkreuz.

These photos show the battery in lager at the edge of a forest. A number of Zeltbahn shelter quarters have been joined to make tents and in the background of one photo is a StuG.III Ausf.E with an 'E' or 'F' painted on the side. The white outlined Balkenkreuz is now filled in with black paint. Some men are wearing mosquito nets over their heads to help protect them from both mosquitos and flies. A keg of beer has attracted a large crowd for a beer ration. Several men stand around a Zündapp KS600 motorcycle combination.

Left: This StuG.III Ausf.D, still carrying the older narrow style Balkenkreuz, has been fitted with a spare track bar on the front of the hull and spare road wheel brackets on the side of the superstructure. This photo provides a clear detail of the mounting bracket and shows that the lifting hook was cut off. Note as well the crossed steel strap brush guards over the lights and electric horn that seemed to be common on some of the batteries vehicles.

Above: Two le.gep.Mun.Tr.Kw. (Sd.Kfz.252) armored ammunition carriers get washed by their crewmen in a shallow river. They were fitted with a Ukw.E.h ultra short-wave receiver and the antenna mount for this can be seen on the roof. They were able to carry 64 rounds of 7.5cm ammunition in the back plus an additional 64 rounds in the Sd.Ah.32 trailer.

Two StuG.III Ausf.D and some transport trucks at rest in a Russian village while the crewmen wait for orders. The vehicle behind has a 'B' painted in white on the engine starter cover plate and also on the side of the radio pannier. It also has the unit emblem painted on the right rear fender. Note the steel post welded to the roof in front of the loader's hatch.

This StuG.III has been so carefully concealed by spruce boughs that it is almost impossible to determine its identification. The only clue is the vertically stowed spare road wheel on the front that could only fit in this location on the StuG.III Ausf.E. The vehicle commander, an Unteroffizier, is scanning the front with his binoculars while sitting on a dead horse.

The StuG.III Ausf.F began to be manufactured in March 1942 and was armed with the more powerful 7.5cm StuK40 L/43. This new one is attached to the headquarters platoon along with the older StuG.III Ausf.D seen in the foreground. It is painted in the second two-tone tropical paint scheme of 2/3 braun RAL 8020 and 1/3 grau RAL 7027 authorized on 25 March 1942.

Another view of the same two vehicles showing the length of the new gun and heavier welded mantlet to good effect. The rest of the vehicle was identical to the StuG.III Ausf.E except for the internal ammunition stowage racks and raised superstructure roof that housed a large fume extraction fan. This is one of the first production batch produced with the L/43 gun that was later upgraded during production to an L/48 gun.

This StuG.III Ausf.F is from the second production batch and features a longer L/48 gun and additional 30mm armor plates welded to the front of the superstructure and hull. The Notek light was relocated to the center of the glacis plate and the two headlights were no longer mounted on the cast tow brackets. The new ventilator can be clearly seen on the roof. The spare track bar on the front also was introduced with this version.

An attempt has been made to hide the shape of these two StuG.III alongside a brick building located in a Russian city, by leaning scrap lumber and debris against them. The front vehicle is another late StuG.III Ausf.F painted in the two-tone tropical scheme with the additional 30mm armor plates welded on.

This is the same StuG.III Ausf.F as in the previous photo but now our unknown soldier is in the picture and has been promoted to Unteroffizier. He also is wearing the Wound Badge in black for one or two wounds and General Assault Badge pinned to his tunic. With the introduction of the long gun, the StuG.III began to see a change in its role on the battlefield from mobile artillery support to an anti-tank role.

Above: The crewmen of this late StuG.III Ausf.F are taking a break after cutting foliage to help conceal their vehicle from Russian aircraft. Unusually, the hubcap on the drive sprocket is missing. This did not become common until late in 1943 when the cap was dropped from production on the StuG.III Ausf.G.

Below: A broken track is repaired on one of the unit's older StuG.III Ausf.D. The right side has been installed backwards but, because of the mud buildup, it's difficult to tell if both sides are the same.

Above Right: Winter has come again on the Eastern Front and our unknown soldier poses in front of the headquarters dugout with some of his comrades. He now has the Iron Cross First Class pinned to his tunic and the ribbon of the East Front Medal, awarded for service on the Eastern Front between 15 November 1941 and 15 April 1942, on his lapel under the ribbon for the Iron Cross Second class.

Right Middle: Two comrades pose in front of the dugout entrance. Both men hold the rank of Unteroffizier, have the General Assault Badge, Wound Badge in black and Iron Cross First Class. The man on the left has his Iron Cross Second Class and East Front Medal ribbons in his lapel buttonhole while the man on the right has a ribbon bar instead.

Above Left: The same two men as in the previous photo but showing the unit emblem for 2./Sturm.Gesch.Abt.189 above the entrance. Both are also wearing the two braid bars on their should straps indicating they are officer aspirants.

One of the men poses for a photo with his late production StuG.III Ausf.F with a new coat of winter whitewash camouflage paint. The vehicle has been fitted with Winterketten tracks, developed in 1942 for use on the Eastern Front. The wider tracks helped lower the ground pressure of the vehicle in deep snow and improved mobility.

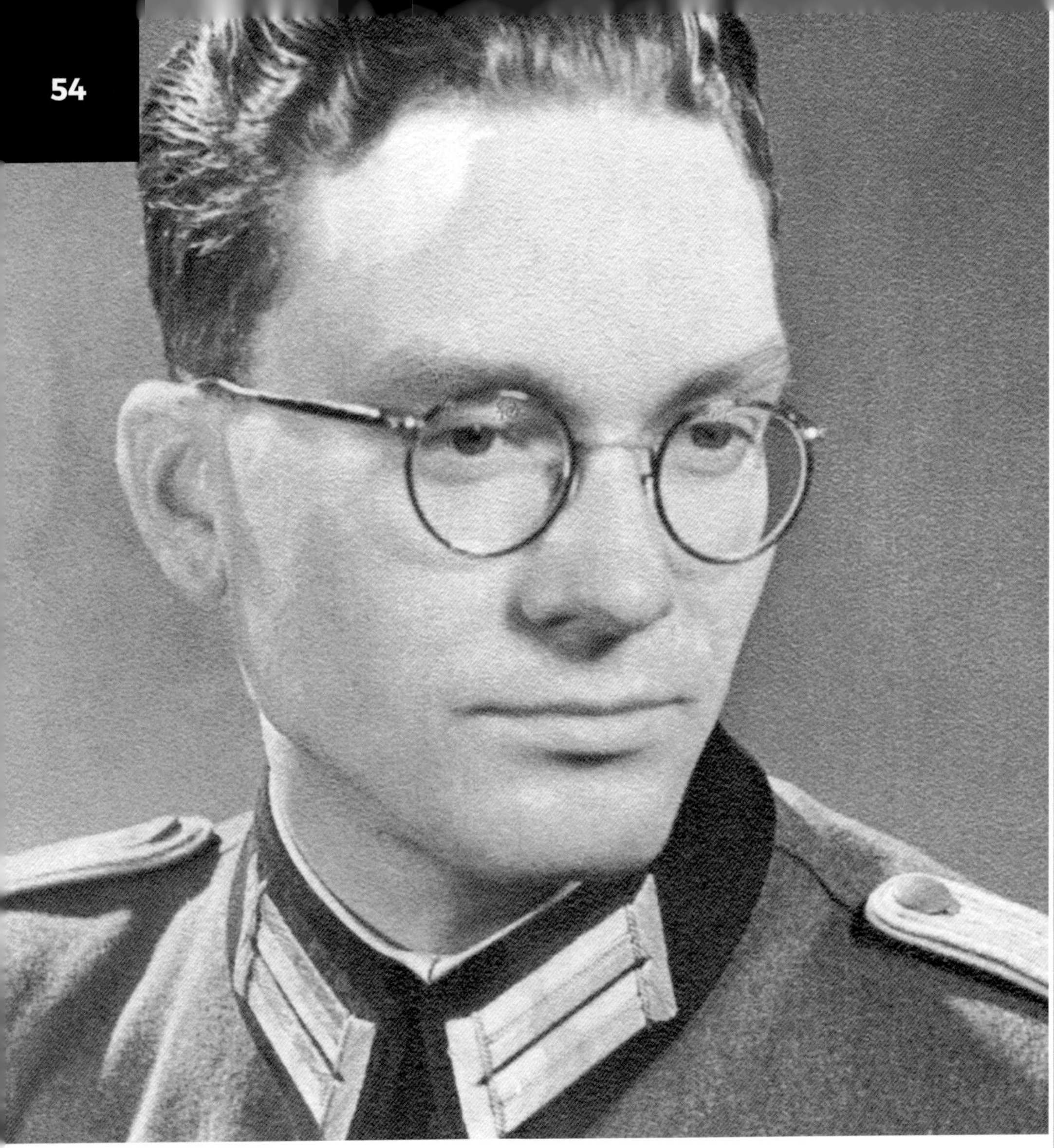

Above Left: Officer candidates, known as Fahnenjunkers, went through a rigorous eight-week training course at a Kriegsschule on the basics of command. Afterwards, they moved to their chosen branch of service. The Wehrmacht operated five Kriegsschulen located in Potsdam, Dresden, München, Hannover and Wiener-Neustadt. In this portrait, our man is wearing new M1936 officer's quality uniform with the dark blue-green collar and shoulder straps of a Leutnant.

Above Right: A studio portrait of our unknown Unteroffizier in his field grey assault gun uniform with the double bar braid of an Offizier Anwärter on his shoulder straps. He is also wearing the Iron Cross First Class beside the General Assault Badge and the Iron Cross Second Class and East Front ribbons in his lapel.

In addition to classroom training, much of the training took place outdoors under the supervision of officer instructors, where the candidates could gain practical knowledge of the tools and equipment available to them. Here we see the candidates undergoing training in the use of the Scherenfernrohr S.F.14.Z.Gi., a scissors telescope invented by Carl Zeiss optics in 1894. They are all wearing one of the variants of the brown leather M1935 report/map case hanging from their belt. Among the candidates is a man with the 'Großdeutschland' cuff band on his M1943 greatcoat.

Above: New Fahnenjunker gather in front of one of the buildings at Kriegsschule Hannover with our man on the right looking away from the camera. Except for one man who is wearing his M1936 service uniform, all are wearing the field grey assault gun uniform. They have been issued with a cartridge pouch worn on the belt although only one is carrying a rifle, a 7.92mm Kar98b. Several of them have also been awarded the marksmanship lanyard. Note as well, the variety of collar patches worn. The metal 'Death's head' emblem was gradually replaced with the standard army collar patches like those worn by the man from 'Großdeutschland'. One man has also been awarded the Individual Tank Destruction Badge worn on his right sleeve.

Right: The gun sight for the leFH 18 consisted of a telescopic sight, the Rundblickfernrohr 32 (Rbl.F.32), mounted to a Zieleinrichtung 34 sighting mechanism that provided an independent line of sight and barrel elevation. Here it has been mounted to a tripod for instructional purposes. Interestingly, the rotating head is pointed away from the target.

Above Right: The 10.5cm leFH 18 M (Mundungbremse or muzzle brake) was an improved version of the leFH 18. In order to obtain greater range, a more powerful propellant was introduced with a resulting increase in recoil forces on the carriage. A muzzle brake was added to help reduce the forces. The wooden spoke wheels were replaced with metal wheels introduced in 1936.

Above: The Fahnenjunker listen intently to their instructor while one of them makes notes at a small desk.
Above Middle: The men, accompanied by their instructor, are gathered in a sturdy wooden bunker for protection and using binoculars to observe the fall of shot during a live fire exercise.
Above and Below Left: More field training in the use of the artillery gun sight. Our man has traded in his M1936 greatcoat for a newer M1943 model with the larger field grey collar and without the turned back cuffs. The man from StuG.Abt. 'Großdeutschland' is speaking on a Feldfernsprecher FF33 field telephone.

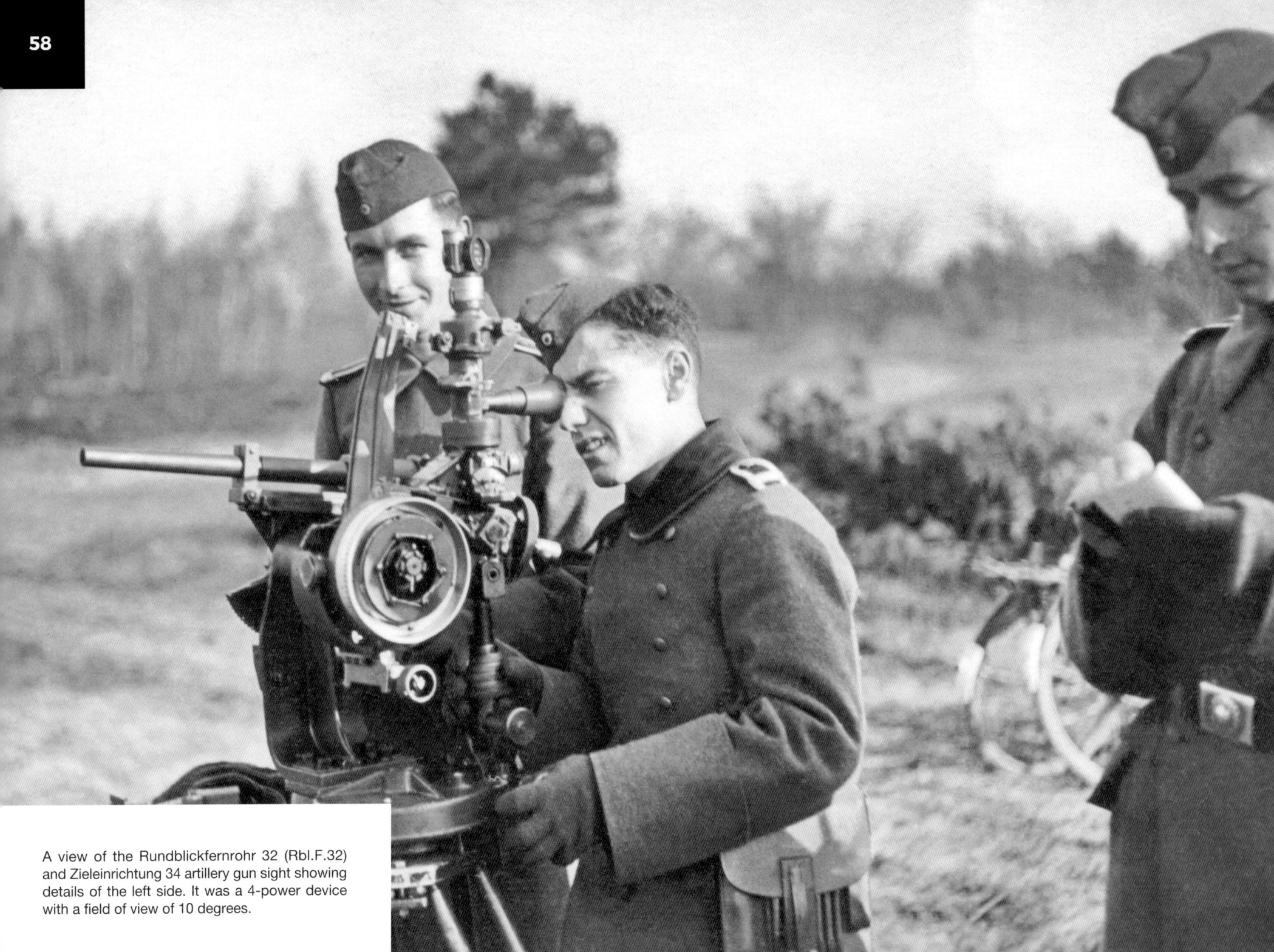

A view of the Rundblickfernrohr 32 (Rbl.F.32) and Zieleinrichtung 34 artillery gun sight showing details of the left side. It was a 4-power device with a field of view of 10 degrees.

One last photo of our Leutnant now wearing standard army collar patches on his field grey assault gun uniform along with his new shoulder straps and officer's leather belt. Unusually, he is no longer wearing his General Assault badge or Wound Badge in black. The man on the right is wearing the Infantry Assault Badge and an SA Sports Badge in bronze while the man in the foreground has the Wound Badge in Silver. Since none of the men are wearing Offizier Anwärter braid on their shoulder straps, it may be an indication that our new Leutnant went on to become an instructor himself.

COMING SOON

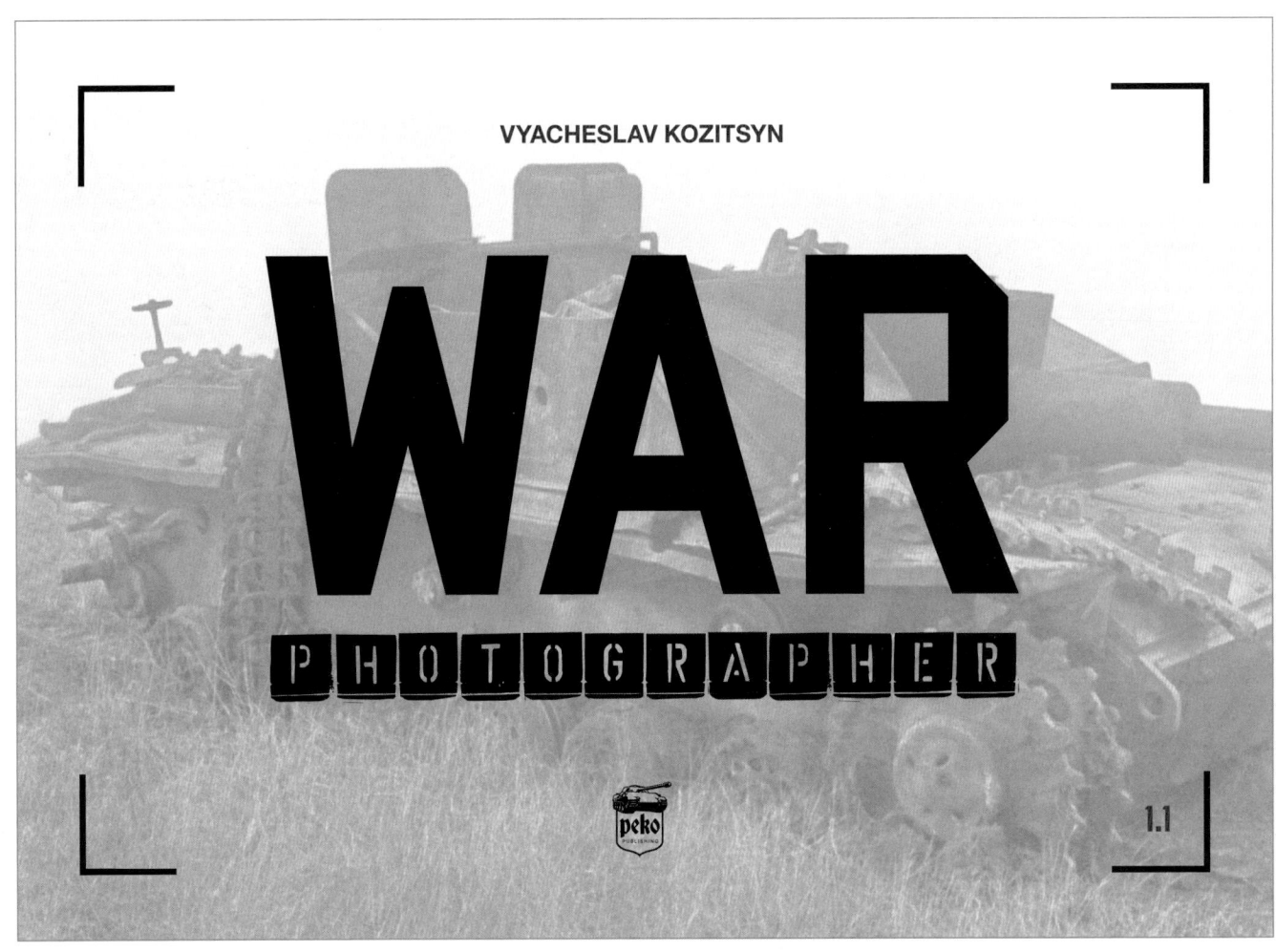